THE HANDBOOK

Jobs-to-be-Done

Practical techniques for improving your application of Jobs-to-be-Done

Chris Spiek & Bob Moesta

with Ervin Fowlkes Jr.

ISBN 978-1-4993-3923-9

Copyright © 2014 by The Re-Wired Group LLC.

All rights reserved. No part of this book may be reproduced in any form or by any electronic or mechanical means without permission in writing from The Re-Wired Group, except by reviewers who may quote brief passages in reviews.

Milkshake cover sketchnote by Mike Rohde – Rohdesign.com

#JTBD

TABLE OF CONTENTS

The Framework	5
Who To Interview	11
Interview Technique	21
Hunting for Energy	33
Note-Taking & Recording	39
Debriefing	43

Appendix

Appendix A – Tips & Techniques	49
Appendix B – Sample Screener Questions	59

Is This Book For You?

How Familiar Are You With Jobs-to-be-Done?

We've written this book for the Jobs-to-be-Done student and practitioner who has a basic grasp of JTBD concepts (Forces Diagram, JTBD Timeline, Interview Process) and wants to strengthen their technique and continue to get better results out of their application of Jobs-to-be-Done.

Not Quite Ready?

There are lots of resources available to help you get caught up on the Jobs-to-be-Done basics. Visit JobstobeDone.org and think about:

- Listening to the JTBD Radio podcast (especially the sample interviews).
- Taking the Online JTBD Course and learning on your own time.
- Attending a Switch Workshop and getting an immersive one-day crash course in Jobs-to-be-Done.

How to Use This Book

The only person who knows what you'll hire this book for is you (but we have our theories). Consider:

- Cramming it to pull out anything you haven't seen before.
- Flipping through it a few minutes before you conduct an interview to review the basics.
- Using it to think through who to interview when starting a project.
- Handing it to a colleague to quickly bring them up-to-speed on JTBD so they can be your interview partner.

#JTBD

SECTION 1

The Framework

#JTBD

The Timeline

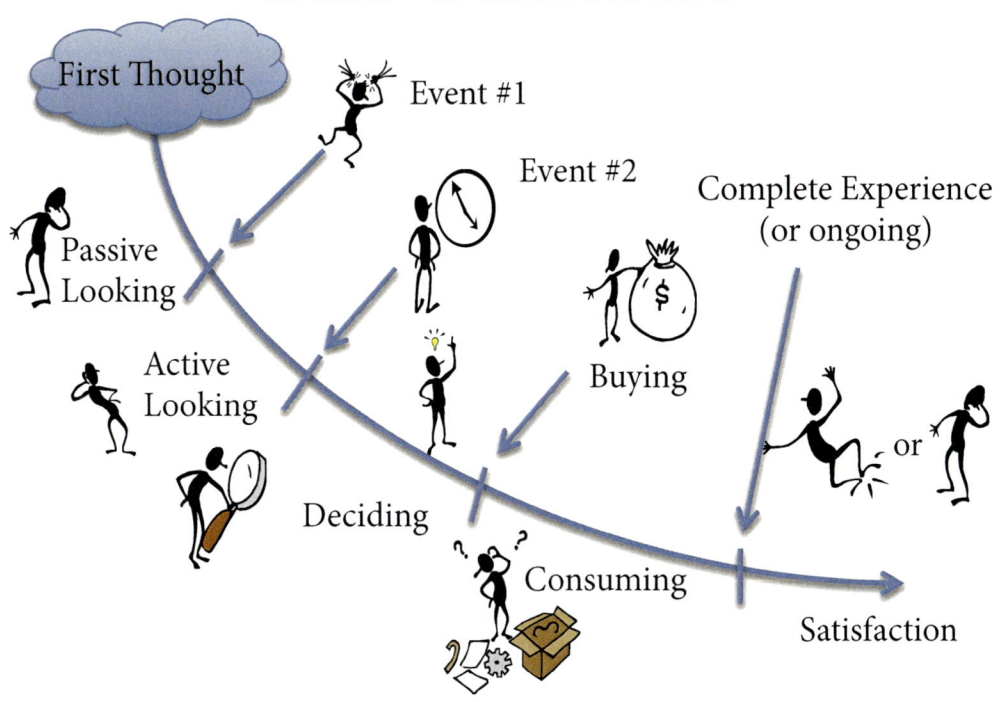

First Thought: *I might need to make progress. Business-as-usual might not be working any more.*

Passive Looking: *I'm not putting in any real energy, but I'm noticing options/solutions that I haven't noticed before.*

Event #1: *I've had enough. This needs to get solved. That event that just happened was dramatic / the energy built up over time and just boiled over.*

Active Looking: *I'm investing energy and time into finding a solution.*

Event #2: *The clock is ticking. I realized that if I don't get it solved by a certain time, it's not going to be good.*

Deciding: *I've narrowed my options to two or three. I understand my criteria.*

Buying: *I've committed to the solution. Paid money. No going back.*

Consuming: *I've used the product or service and understand if it does the job.*

Satisfaction: *Did it help me make progress or not?*

#JTBD

#JTBD

The Forces of Progress

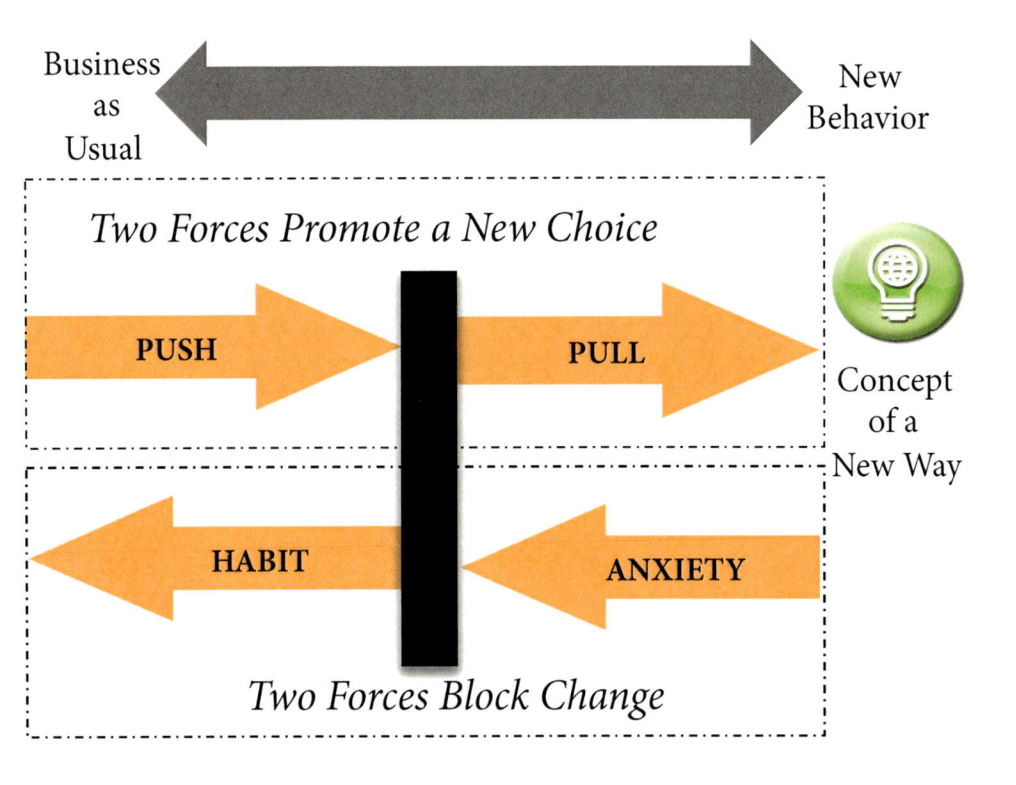

Business as Usual ↔ **New Behavior**

Two Forces Promote a New Choice

PUSH → ← PULL → Concept of a New Way

Two Forces Block Change

← HABIT ← ANXIETY

Push: The forward-pushing energy related to my current situation. I need to make it better.

Pull: The forward-pulling energy related to a possible solution. Can this help me make progress?

Anxiety: The progress-blocking energy related to a possible solution. Will it work? Can I figure it out?

Habit: The progress-blocking energy related to my current situation. What I do now isn't so bad. I'm familiar with my current solution.

#JTBD

#JTBD

SECTION 2

Who to Interview

Why Worry So Much About Recruiting?

Conducting interviews takes time. Not just the two or three days that you'll spend interviewing (if you're doing 10 to 15 interviews), but the time spent designing the screener, recruiting people, scheduling the interviews, and sending out the incentives to the participants after the interviews are completed. In order to make sure that your time is well spent, you need to make sure that you're talking to the right people.

Because we're focused on *why they bought this product*, we need to make sure that the people actually have a story that they can tell us. People who don't have a story about why they bought come in many forms:

- **They bought the product too long ago.**
    - They might have a good story buried in there somewhere, but getting to it can be difficult after too much time has passed.
- **They got the product as a gift.**
    - The product just landed in their lap! There's a job there, but it's the job of the person who purchased the gift to give to them.
- **They weren't the ultimate decision maker.**
    - Products purchased by married couples sometimes can be tricky and fall under this category, but we can ask questions in our screener to figure out who had more influence over budget, timing, and the consideration set.

#JTBD

The effects of a bad recruiting process will be apparent when you start talking to these people. You'll wrestle to find any of the points in the timeline, and it will feel like none of the four forces acted on them.

#JTBD

Recruiting for Consumer Products

Which groups of people do we want to talk to?
- Group A) People who recently purchased our product.
- Group B) People who recently left our product (bought something else or just stopped using it).
- Group C) People who recently purchased a competing product.

Make sure that each participant meets the basic criteria:
- They were the decision maker / buyer.
- The bought within a certain time period (recently!).
- They actually purchased it (not a free trial, gift).
- They used the product since they purchased it.

Consider recruiting a mix of:
- People who heard about it from different sources (friends, advertisements).
- People who bought from different channels (in a store, online).
- People who used it differently after buying it (used it every day, used it once per month).
- People from different demographic segments, if you have a hunch that it effects the purchase (age, married, kids, retired).
- People who bought with a discount, a coupon, or paid full price.

#JTBD

Recruiting for Business-to-Business Products

When recruiting for business-to-business (B2B) products and services it's important to remember that businesses don't buy things. **People buy things.**

Although the purchasing process may involve a number of people with different perspectives and goals (CFO: Budget, CTO: Security, COO: Implementation Resources), each of these people will ultimately have a situation that they're in that will define job-requirements.

CTO: *We just had a security breach last month, anything we buy now needs to be air-tight.*
COO: *Our strategy this year includes improving our efficiency metric. Anything I'm investing capital in needs to influence that.*

Our focus when trying to understand jobs in the B2B space is to not only understand the jobs that each player in the purchasing process is trying to get done, but the system in which these players operate.

#JTBD

The first few interviews that we conduct (up to 10 or sometimes more) will help us understand the landscape of how our product is purchased:

- What roles/job titles are involved?
- When is it purchased by an individual and when is it purchased as a team?
- How do the roles interact to shape up what they're looking for.
- How is the final purchase decision made?

#JTBD

Unpacking the B2B Purchase Process

In order to understand the landscape of a B2B purchase, we want to draw on a number of data sources:

1. Our knowledge of the space (but not our *assumptions* about how it operates).
2. The responses that we get after we send out our screener.
    1. How many people bought it alone? (had complete control of budget, timing, selection of the solution).
    2. How many people bought it as part of a group that they led (got input, but they made the ultimate decision)?
    3. Who answered the screener and said they led the group or had the final say in the purchase (what was their role / job title?)
3. The first few interviews that we conduct.
    1. What players in the system first brought up the idea of something new?
    2. How did the other players advance or hold back the story?
    3. Who was in charge of moving the purchase over the finish line?

#JTBD

B2B Screener Question Example

1. So let's get started. For your organization, were you the person who:

	Yes (solely)	Yes (as part of a group/team)	No
Had the final say in what type of Customer Relationship Management (CRM) system to purchase?	○	○	○
Was responsible for evaluating different solutions before a purchase was made?	○	○	○
Had control of how much you could spend on a solution?	○	○	○

The screener question above provides us with basic information about the person's role in the purchase process.

Filter this information when conducting your initial recruit to get a good mix of different perspectives on the process. Recruit people who answered some version of "Yes" to at least one of the questions.

#JTBD

Incentivizing Interview Participants

If you pay people to talk to you, won't they just tell you what they think you want to hear?

This premise may hold true for many research methods, but it's not applicable to Jobs-to-be-Done. What we want to hear is the story of how they shopped for and bought the product that they bought. Remember, we don't have an angle or preconceived notion that we're trying to validate. We just want their story.

If at the beginning of the interview the person you're interviewing feels like they need to give you the the answers you're looking for, they'll quickly realize that you don't have an angle, just based on the questions that you're asking them.

Tips on Incentives
- Consider using gift cards as incentives (Amazon, Vias, and American Express all work great).
- A $50 to $100 gift card is usually enough to get consumers to talk to you for an hour. You may need to go over $100 for business-to-business projects.
- Avoid giving away your product as an incentive ("Two Months Free for talking to us!")

The decision to incentivize participants is ultimately up to you. Our position has been that if I'm asking someone for their time, I should compensate them for it.

#JTBD

#JTBD

SECTION 3

Interview Technique

Starting the Interview

Make Them Feel Comfortable!

The introduction is all about the participant!

Here are the topics that you need to make sure you cover:
1. Make them feel comfortable:
   - "There are no right or wrong answers."
2. Downplay the importance:
   - "This is just early research before the 'real research' starts."
3. Give them an out:
   - "If you can't remember something, that's okay."

A Sample Intro

Make it your own voice, and smile when you say this:

Thanks for coming in and taking the time to talk to us! So, we're doing some research around how people shop for and buy [product]. But before we go and do the big, formal research project, we wanted to just get a handful of people in the room to talk about the last time they shopped for a [product]. We don't know a whole lot about [product] and it's helping us to just hear how people talk about it.

So this is just going to be a really casual conversation. There aren't any right or wrong answers, since it's really just your story about how you came to buy a [product].

If you can't remember a detail that's fine, and if you want to change your answers at any point, that's okay too.

Continue on and add in the documentary metaphor (on the following page).

#JTBD

The Documentary Metaphor

The best way to think about this is like we're filming a documentary about how people have shopped for [product] over the last 30 years..

We want all the details around when you first started thinking about buying the [product], when you made the decision, and then when you started using it and experiencing it for the first time.

So we'll ask really broad questions, and then there will be some situations where we'll slow down and ask for all kinds of crazy details: who were you with, what time of day it was, was the store crowded or empty, things like that. It's like we're trying to film the scene for our documentary and we need all of the detail to set the scene.

I know it's kind of goofy but just bear with me. [SMILE!]
Sound good?   Okay, let's get started …

#JTBD

Asking the First Question

At the beginning of an interview you have a lot to remember:

- Introduce yourself.
- Smile!
- Do the intro.
- Introduce the documentary metaphor.
- Start the interview.

That last one trips a lot of people up, so we'll make it easy.

This is the first question to ask:
"So we know you bought a [general product name], but what exactly did you buy, and where did you buy it?

After the First Question

The answer to your first question should let loose a torrent of follow-up questions in your brain. Here are some examples.

Well I don't remember exactly when ...
- Hmm ... do you remember if it was a weekday or weekend?
- Was it before Christmas of this year? After New Years? Before the holidays started?
- Was it in the morning? In the evening?

I bought it at a store.
- Was the store crowded or empty?
- Did anyone help you? Did they come right up to you or wait a while?
- Who was with you? Your spouse? Your kids?

I bought it online.
- Oh, were you at work or at home?
- How long did you look around before you clicked buy?
- Where in your house were you?
- What was your husband doing while you were online?
- Was the TV on? Did you have music playing?

#JTBD

Reacting to Fatigue

Even though we have that torrent of questions around the moment that they purchased the product, the person you're interviewing might not have all of the answers yet.

Train yourself to feel their energy start to drop. If they're not straining to think of the answers to your questions, you need to jump to a new topic.

When they start to just throw up their arms and say, "I *really* just can't remember (or hopefully shortly before that happens if you're good), it's time to jump to the first thought.

Here's what to ask:

"So tell me, how did all of this come about? What were you using before you bought this [product]? Do you remember the first time you thought about buying a [product]?"

Getting to the *First Thought*

It's difficult to remember the very first time you thought about making progress in some way. Usually the first thing an interview participant tells you is the First Thought really isn't the first thought.

Often times when we're a half hour into an interview we'll hear something like "… oh I remember why I started looking!" Listen for those moments.

Now let's look at how you can work on it from both directions in time.

#JTBD

First Thought

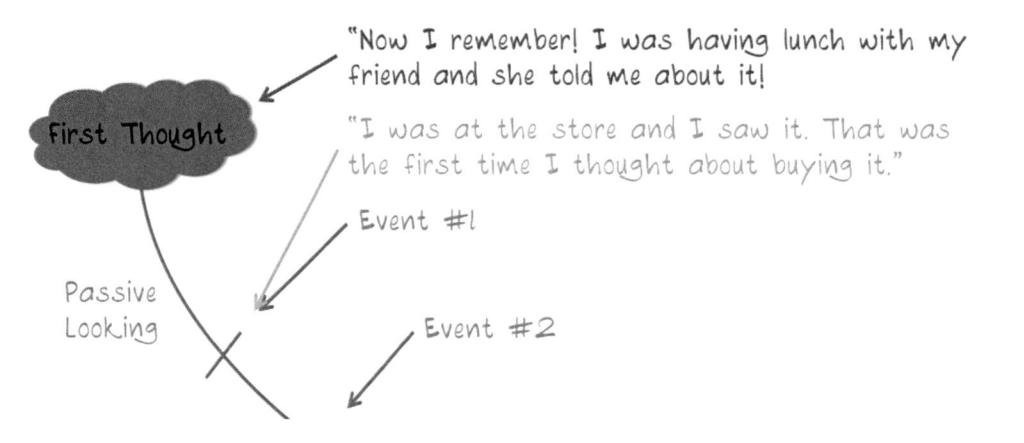

"Now I remember! I was having lunch with my friend and she told me about it!"

"I was at the store and I saw it. That was the first time I thought about buying it."

Event #1

Passive Looking

Event #2

Working it Backwards
- "Tell me about the first time you had the thought: 'I need to find a new solution.'"
- What events led up to that moment? Search for causality.

Working it Forward
- "Tell me about the old_____ (mattress, cell phone, laundry detergent). Why didn't you buy the same thing again?"

#JTBD

Building Rapport

The faster you can build a close connection to the interview participant, the higher the likelihood that they'll relax and focus on thinking about their answers to the questions that you're asking.

Always ask for the names of the other characters in the story. If they're married, ask for their spouse's name. The same goes for kids and pets!

Don't be afraid to relate: "Yeah that's happened to me too." Just don't do it so much so they can answer your questions with "well you know – you've been there."

Thanks to the folks at Appiphony for the illustration: appiphony.com

#JTBD

Conducting Practice Interviews

Practice is an important part of learning to do Jobs-to-be-Done interviews. It's also important to pick the right topics to explore.

The goal is to help you refine your technique while avoiding overly complex topics.

Find someone to talk to who has:
- Made the purchase within the last 90 days.
- Purchased something over $100 (new phone, laptop, camera, etc).
- Purchased the item for the first time (not just a refill).
- Make sure it wasn't a gift (one they received or purchased for someone else).
- Something that they struggled with (spent more than a day thinking about purchasing it).

For your first few interviews, think about talking to co-workers, friends, or family.

… SECTION …

4

Hunting for Energy

Energy is What Makes JTBD Different

There are plenty of research and product development techniques that are good at helping us understand *what* consumers are doing and what products they're using.

What makes Jobs-to-be-Done so different (and so powerful) is that we're always looking for *why* consumers do what they do. It's the *why* that always takes us back to the concept of energy.

The consumer didn't just black out one morning, drive to the store, and purchase the product. Something happened that caused the purchase.

Because most of us are product people, we get caught up in the product:

> *Tell me about your old mattress. How did it compare to the new one? Was it softer, harder, lumpier? Now tell me about the mattress you have now ...*[1]

---

[1] *Listen to the Mattress Interview at http://bit.ly/jtbdmattress*

#JTBD

The truth is, I don't care about the mattress. I care about the situation that was in that caused him to think about abandoning the status-quo:

> *It got to a point where I would be up at 4am searching online for mattresses because my back hurt so bad that I couldn't sleep.*

Holy cow! There's some energy! I can sell to that. I can craft marketing messages around it.

#JTBD

Finding Your Way to the Energy

In order to find our way to the energy, we need to start our conversation with the participant and begin to zoom in. Below is a diagram that we use to outline the questions (tricks) that we can use to start at a high-level and begin to zoom in on the Jobs-to-be-Done timeline: the moment when they had the first thought that they needed to make progress, all the way through purchasing and using the product.

At the beginning of the interview we don't know where that timeline is, and we have to set out to find it. Everything before it is status-quo (normal behavior) and everything after it is status-quo (the new habits/behaviors have been set / progress has been made).

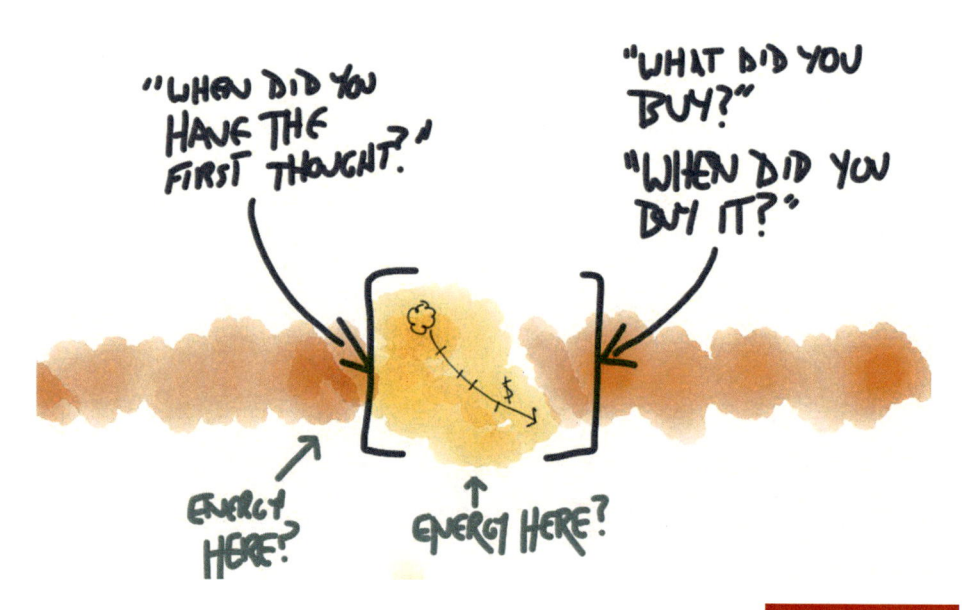

#JTBD

Bracket the Story

When you're trying to locate the story, start by trying to set the right bracket:

What exactly did you buy? Do you remember the brand? What else do you remember about it? (model/features?)

When did you buy it? Was it a weekend or weekday? Do you remember if it was before Thanksgiving or after?

Then move to the left bracket (this one is much trickier to find):

When did you have the first thought that you needed something new? Do you remember a moment when you said to yourself, 'this mattress just isn't cutting it?'

From there it's up to you to decide if you believe them or if you need to keep moving back in time (the first thought that they shared with you sometimes isn't really the first thought—it's just the one that they remember most easily and you need to keep probing).

#JTBD

Practice Your Empathy

Understanding the energy requires you to be empathetic of their situation.

> *It got to a point where I would be up at 4am searching online for mattresses because my back hurt so bad that I couldn't sleep.*

Do you have enough resolution with that statement to be empathetic? If not, dig in and ask some clarifying questions:

- *So how often was this happening? Was it every day?*
- *It must have been terrible to go through that. Was it a dull pain or a stabbing pain?*
- *Did it just happen all of a sudden one day, or did it build up over time?*

The more you can learn about the nature of the energy, the easier it will be to understand the *why* and to compare and contrast different consumer's stories against each other.

For example:

- People with sharp stabbing back pain that came on all of a sudden all bought within a week and paid 50% more than other consumers!
- People with dull pain that built up over the years all took 8 months or more to buy, and sought out the best deal they could find.

#JTBD

SECTION 5

Note Taking & Recording

Ask to Record the Interview

It always feels strange asking someone if you can record them. However, we can honestly say that we've done it hundreds if not thousands of times, and can probably count on one hand the times that people have said, "no."

Recording the interview is critical for a number of reasons:
- It allows you to focus on what questions you want to ask, not on capturing absolutely everything the person says.
- It enables you to easily share the story with your coworkers, your boss, etc. If you need to drive a point home, there's nothing better than sharing a 15 second clip of an actual consumer making your point in their words.

After you do your intro, just ask:
Is it okay if I record this interview?

If the topic is especially sensitive, ask.
I'd like to record this interview. It's just for our internal records. We're not going to share it or anything. Is that okay?

It's very rare that someone will turn you down (but it does happen).

#JTBD

Start With a Blank Timeline

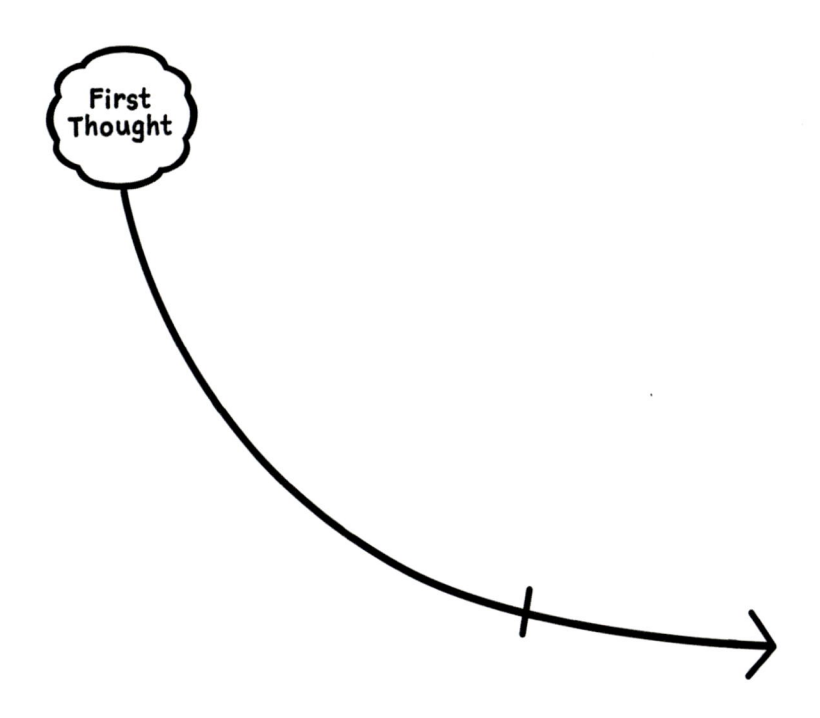

(First Thought)

Use your notebook to mark important moments in time. Remember, you have the recording of the interview so you don't need to worry about writing down every single detail that they mention.

Start with one mark on the line that signifies the moment that they bought the product that you're talking to them about.

As they mention events in the story, add marks and record the date that they say. This will help you to keep the story straight in your head, and allow you to glance down quickly to find gaps or areas that you need to explore more.

#JTBD

SECTION 6

Debriefing

The Clock is Ticking!

The one hour period after you complete an interview is arguably even more important than the interview itself.

Because interviews are often emotional and usually incredibly rich with detail, you'll walk out of each one with three types of knowledge:

1. **HOLY COW Insights:** These are ideas that you can't wait to discuss with your team and act on (usually just one or two per interview).
2. **Interesting Comments:** These are things that the interviewee said that you might not have heard before and that you need to take note of.
3. **Necessary Details:** These are the rest of the details to the story that are just as valuable, but might not seem so until you start to compare them to other interviews (did they buy online or in a store? Did they use a coupon? Were they referred by a friend?)

Because it's so tempting to spend the hour after an interview talking about the Holy Cow Insights (and then miss all the rest of the important details), we've created a de-brief process that gives structure to the time following an interview and ensures that all of the details are captured.

#JTBD

The Debrief Worksheet

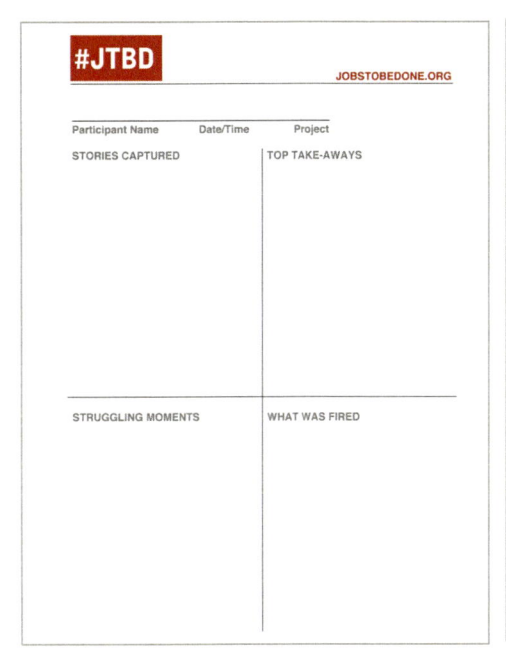

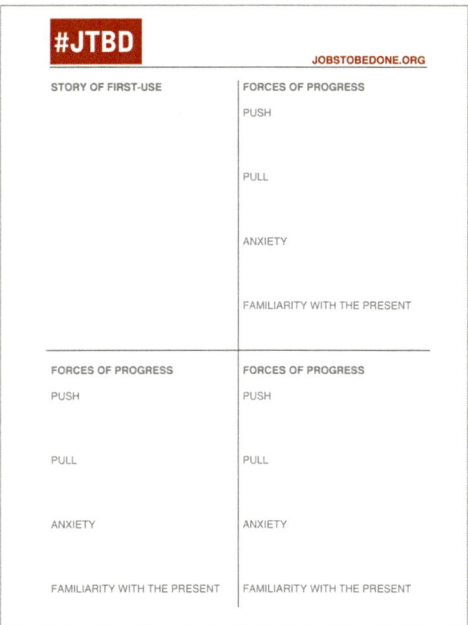

Download a PDF version of the worksheet above at: http://bit.ly/jtbdpostworksheet

- When the interview concludes, and after the team gets through their first two or three minutes of chatter, set a timer for 10 minutes..
- Let the team know that this is *quiet time*, and that everyone should be filling out the sheet with what they heard.
- When the ten minutes is up, begin your discussion by going around the room. Have one team member share a top take-away (we like to record it on a whiteboard or flip-chart paper) and continue until the team feels like all of the insights and details have been discussed.

The Worksheet Elements

Stories Captured

Bullet point the stories that you heard. What products/solutions did they buy? Did you get the story of them learning about the product and purchasing it (switching)? Did you get the story of the first time they used it? List each one.

Top Take-Aways

As you think about the interview and the project as a whole, what were the most useful points that will be important to the project?

Struggling Moments

What were they struggling with? Why did they want to make progress?

What Was Fired

What did they fire when they switched to the new product(s)? List everything that you can think of. Was it fired in every situation, or just some?

Story of First Use

Roughly outline the story and experience they had using the product for the first time (using bullet points). What did they expect before they use it? Did they wait a while after they purchased the product? How did they decide when and how to use it?

#JTBD

Forces of Progress
- Before they purchased the product, what forces were acting on them? (do this for each story/switch that you heard)
- Pull: How did the idea of the new product motivate them or pull them toward it?
- Push: What was going on in their lives that was pushing them to make progress?
- Anxiety: What about the new product were they worried about?
- Familiarity / Habit of the Present: What allegiances did they have to the "old way of doing things" that was hard for them to break?

#JTBD

#JTBD

Appendix A

Tips & Tricks

Let Them Get Their Thoughts Out

If you're working with a product or market that people are really passionate about, plan on encountering some unique challenges when conducting interviews.

The people you talk to will want to praise your product, give you feedback on what you should fix, or tell you what you could add to the product to make it even better.

As a Jobs-to-be-Done practitioner, you know why you're conducting the interviewer. *There's JTBD gold in this person's story, and I need to find it!* It's always tempting to suppress their comments and focus them on the story of how they purchased the product.

The trick is to **let them get it all out of their head at the beginning of the interview.** That way we're free to move on to the story that we're focused on.

- *I love your product but I use a separate product to do _____. If you combined them you guys would make a ton of money!*
  - *That's great feedback. Thanks for telling us about how you use it!*
- *I've had so much trouble doing _____ with your product. It's a pain!*
  - *I'm sorry to hear that. I'll have someone from our support team contact you so we can get that sorted out.*

#JTBD

If we cut them off and try to refocus them by saying something like, "that's really interesting but what I'm really here to talk to you about is …" we're essentially asking them to answer our questions while they hold those great ideas in their head so they can tell us about them later.

Dummy Up!

By now you're starting to understand that getting to a Job-to-be-Done is all about connecting the dots that paint a picture of causality.

We want to stress in this tip that you shouldn't ever try to connect two dots, when it's easier to just **ask a question.**

When you ask a question and get an answer, check your thought process. If you catch yourself thinking, "Yeah that makes perfect sense," **STOP**.

Do you really have the full picture, or are you better off saying "I'm not sure I completely understand. Can you tell me more about why you did that?"

You'll be amazed at what you'll discover and how often your assumptions are incorrect.

#JTBD

Connecting the Wrong Dots

We've all been in interviews where the participant just starts to agree with you and give short simple answers.

Getting yourself out of that trap is easy. You do it by *connecting the wrong dots.*

Start by recapping a part of the story that you don"t have complete clarity on ("Why on this specific evening were they dedicating so much time to shopping online for this product?").

Instead of trying to dig deeper and risk getting another simple answer, connect the wrong dots and hopefully force them to correct you.

You: "So your family was away that evening, and that's why you could spend so much time shopping?"

Them: "No! They were there with me, but I had a trip coming up three days later, and if I didn't order in time it wouldn't make it to me before I left!"

#JTBD

Rules for an Interview Partner

Having a partner to conduct interviews with is a fantastic luxury, but very few of us have people around us who are completely versed in the Jobs-to-be-Done framework.

Before you go it alone, consider pulling someone in to be your partner and bringing them up to speed quickly on the framework.

Here is your 20-minute onboarding process:
1. Explain the Forces of Progress diagram to them.
2. Walk them through the timeline and explain to them that it's the basic outline of what you're going to try to uncover during the interview.
3. Explain to them that their role is to keep the conversation going if you need to think of your next question.
4. Give them some question guidelines so they have ideas on what to ask about:
   - Ask anything related to the situation that we're talking about at the moment. For example, if they're describing their experience in the store, ask about it, but don't pull us out of the moment to ask about how they felt when they got home and started using the product.
   - Stay away from product-specific questions like: What do you like most about the product? What do you like least? It's a wormhole that is difficult to get out of once you're in it.

#JTBD

Avoiding a Psychological Evaluation

We've discovered while teaching Jobs-to-be-Done that discovering the emotional energy related to a purchase can be a double-edged sword.

It's powerful as it relates to understanding the causality of a purchase, but it can also be incredibly cathartic for both the interviewer and the interviewee.

We've seen interviewers become so enamored by the consumer's behavior that they start asking questions like:

- *You're so passionate about this product! What else are you passionate about to this extent?*
- *It sounds like this was a snap-decision. Do you always make quick purchase decisions like this?*

Resist this urge at all cost. As fascinating as it may be to understand someone's behavior at a broader level, remember, it's not what we're here to do. We're conducting an interview to understand why they bought what they bought at that exact moment in time, and what else they considered to get the job done.

#JTBD

Their Story. Their Language.

For most of us it's hard to understand just how close to our products and industries we actually are. We understand the technology at an intimate level and we expect that others have at least a fraction of the understanding that we do. **We're wrong.**

All of the brand names, model numbers, acronyms, feature names, even product categories that we rattle off every day in casual conversations with our colleagues is a useless and foreign language to the majority of consumers.

In addition to uncovering the causality of the purchase, the interview is a great opportunity to understand what they know about our product and how they talk about it. Here are some rules to get the most out of this aspect of the interview:

- Don't correct their language. If they say, "camera that I can change the lens on," don't say, "Yeah, DSLR."
- Don't add hiring criteria just because it's important to you (you may get an answer, but you won't know if it's important to them).
    - "How many megapixels was the camera?"
- Dummy up and probe on every opportunity. Even if it's an industry that you've worked in for the last 30 years.
    - "I have no idea what that's called. What do you call it?"

This is all great language that you can use to message and market your product.

#JTBD

Unlocking Memories

After you do a couple of interviews, you'll start to get pretty used to hearing, "I just can't remember."

While there are no fool-proof techniques to making someone remember (recruiting good candidates helps!), there are some tips that can trigger memories.

Remember that we have our documentary metaphor. If the participant insists that they can't remember, *gently* start asking some questions "around" the situation.

"I know I was on my laptop shopping online, but I have no idea what day it was."

- Where were you? At the office? At home?
- Was the door to your office open or closed?
- Was the TV on? Did you have music playing?
- Was it sunny out? Cold? Raining?
- Was it during the day or late at night?

By asking questions "around" the situation that we're examining, we can often get the brain to zero in on the memory that we're searching for.

#JTBD

Limit Your Note Taking

Some of the best interviews we've seen have been conducted by people who take very limited notes.

The truth is, they're completely focused on:
1. The interviewee.
2. The story.
3. The next question they're going to ask.
4. The gaps that they need to fill in to get a complete picture.

If you find yourself feeling uncomfortable or anxious because there are long gaps between your questions or if you feel like you're scrambling to record every little detail of every interview, challenge yourself to take less notes on the next one.

Write down only what you need to get the timeline right (what events happened in what order), and to figure out the gaps that you need to fill in.

Remember, you always have the recording that you can go back to, and if you have a team listening in you have their recollection of the interview to fall back on as well.

#JTBD

Appendix B

Sample Recruiting Questions

Sample B2C Questions

- Is this the first time you've bought a [PRODUCT/SERVICE]?
- When you purchased it, did you have a coupon, was it on sale, or was it full price?
- When did you buy the [PRODUCT/SERVICE]? (approximate is fine)
- Where did you buy the [PRODUCT/SERVICE]?
- When you bought the [PRODUCT/SERVICE], did you make the decision alone, or with someone else? (if so, who?)
- Did you buy it for yourself, or as a gift for someone else?
- If it was for someone else, what is your relationship to the recipient?
- If you bought it as a gift, what was the occasion?
- How did you first hear about the [PRODUCT/SERVICE]?
- How many [PRODUCT/SERVICE]s do you currently own?
- When you bought this [PRODUCT/SERVICE], what other options did you consider?
- How long did you shop, or look around for options before you made your purchase?

#JTBD

End the screener with:
1. Only two more questions. We're looking for a few people to participate in a more thorough conversation about their experience with their [PRODUCT/SERVIC] (about 45 minutes long). If you're picked, you'll be compensated for your participation. Would you be willing to talk more about your experience?
2. If you answered yes to the question above, please list your name, email address, and contact phone number so I can reach out to you.

#JTBD

Sample B2B Questions

- Tell me about your role in using [PRODUCT/SERVICE] within your organization.
- Tell me about your role in setting up the [PRODUCT/SERVICE] for your organization.
- About how often do you use the [PRODUCT/SERVICE]?
- How many people in your organization use the [PRODUCT/SERVICE] regularly?
- What are some of the roles / job titles of the people in your organization that use the [PRODUCT/SERVICE]?
- What is your role in the organization?
- How long have you been with the company?
- How long have you been in your current role?
- How many employees work at the company?
- What industry is the company in?
- What other [PRODUCT/SERVICE]s have you used in the past?

End the screener with:
1. Only two more questions. We're looking for a few people to participate in a more thorough conversation about their experience with their [PRODUCT/SERVIC] (about 45 minutes long). If you're picked, you'll be compensated for your participation. Would you be willing to talk more about your experience?
2. If you answered yes to the question above, please list your name, email address, and contact phone number so I can reach out to you.

#JTBD

#JTBD

Looking For

More Help?

Here are a few ways to connect with us

Chris Spiek
cspiek@rewiredinc.com
@chriscbs

Bob Moesta
bmoesta@rewiredinc.com
@bmoesta

Ervin Fowlkes
efowlkes@rewiredinc.com
@ervinfowlkes

About the Authors

Chris Spiek

I'm a Partner and Co-Founder at The Re-Wired Group, an innovation consultancy focused on enabling R&D functions within Fortune 500 companies to develop products that consumers love to buy and use.

Through the use of short, fast consulting engagements, and the incredibly popular one-day Switch Workshop , I teach people how to think differently about their consumers, and show them how to understand what motivates people to shop and buy.

I've been studying, refining, and applying Jobs-to-be-Done across a wide variety of industries for over 10 years (software, education, consumer-packaged-goods, healthcare, and e-commerce to name a few).

Tune into Jobs-to-be-Done Radio, on iTunes each week to hear Bob Moesta and I apply JTBD to different product development and marketing challenges (and hear about how companies like 37signals, Meetup and others are applying the JTBD framework!).

#JTBD

About the Authors

Bob Moesta

I am an Innovator (JTBD Method), a Product Developer (+1000 new products), a Businessman (5 Startups), a Mentor, a Student, and a Citizen. I believe there are more opportunities and need for change at hand today than there has been in a long time. The opportunity for change is really about personal INNOVATION. It is time for the world to take full advantage of the over-supply of technology and learn to INNOVATE by applying this technology in new and unique ways.

I have been blessed with the opportunity to work directly with some great mentors in Clayton Christensen, Dr. Genichi Taguchi, W. Edwards Deming, and many others.

After some urging by Clay Christensen at Harvard Business School in 2009, Chris Spiek and I started The Re-Wired Group in Detroit, Michigan.

I know we can not do this alone. I am passionate about conversing, sharing, and learning.

#JTBD